BEYOND THE LAUNCH

HOW BUILDING A QUALITY PRODUCT CAN SET YOUR BUSINESS UP FOR SUCCESS

PHELYX O'DAVID

This book is dedicated to young Entrepreneurs who are enthusiastic about solving problems globally.

ACKNOWLEDGMENTS

Thank you to all those who have helped me to grow and learn about life. My family, teachers, mates, friends, and those in my neighbourhood.

TABLE OF CONTENT

INTRODUCTION

I like to begin by briefly telling a story shared with me some time ago by my lecturer (in the Principles of Management class). According to him, a young entrepreneur excited about his big idea for a new product got his business off the ground and hurriedly assembled a team to launch without adequate testing and development.

Not so long after he kicked off, the product hit a host of problems, and glitches and frustration set in for the early adopters. Blinded by his eagerness to make a profit, the young entrepreneur ignored feedback from customers and advisors and forgot that profit-making is the act of solving problems.

Over time, the business began to stagger because the desperation to keep the company alive was built on some personal canons and emotions. He used the business funds for personal expenses without accounting for them adequately, after all, he who owns the business, owns the money. He neglected the resolution of the core problems working against the product, rather, he focused on making quick sales and profits. But again, how does he solve the problem when he does not know it?

Eventually, the business came crumbling, leaving the entrepreneur with irredeemable regrets. He realized too late that his impatience, lack of attention to the product's problems, and obsession with making a profit before solving problems had been his downfall.

This cautionary tale serves as a reminder that rushing to market without a solid product can have devastating consequences. Entrepreneurs must take the time to invest in quality development, listen to feedback, and prioritize the long-term success of their business over short-term gains. What the psychologists like Walter Mischel and Sigmund Freud referred to as delayed gratification.

In this article, we want to consider the importance of building scalable, quality, solid, strong and credible products.

CHAPTER 1

BUILDING A STRONG FOUNDATION

The Bible confirms it that, when the foundation is destroyed, even the righteous ones can do nothing.

Building a strong foundation through quality product development is crucial for the long-term success of any business. This process involves thorough research and planning, careful design and engineering, and rigorous testing and evaluation to ensure that the final product meets customer needs and expectations. In other words, it involves a systematic approach to creating a product that

1. **meets customer needs (solving problems)**
2. **stands out in the market (visibility, outstanding)**
3. **provides value to the business (revenue)**

The choice of customer needs as first on the list is intentionally deliberate for the purpose of this piece and of course, the true understanding of starting a business.

The foregoing informs me that quality product development begins with a deep understanding of customer needs and market trends. This includes conducting market research, analyzing consumer behaviour, and identifying opportunities for innovation. Once a viable product concept is developed, it is critical to define product requirements, set clear goals and objectives, and establish a detailed project plan

Quality product development also involves considering factors such as cost, scalability, and sustainability, to ensure that the product can be produced, and deployed efficiently and will remain relevant in the market over time.

With 'quality' as the watchword, every stage of the development process must be rigorously tested, fine-tuned, and continuously evaluated with ongoing feedback from necessary stakeholders. Building a strong foundation through quality product development ensures that a product meets the needs of the target market, is reliable and user-friendly, and is designed for scalability and growth. It makes no sense to build a product with such a short-sightedness for timing and change because those are the two inevitable realities that remain unpredictable yet must come to pass in the lifespan of every business whether we like it or not.

By investing in quality product development, businesses can establish themselves as leaders in their industries, build a loyal customer base, and ultimately achieve sustainable growth and profitability.

Meets Customer Needs (Solving Problems)

Meeting customer needs, or solving problems, is a critical core value for building a strong and quality product. At the heart of any successful business is the ability to understand and meet customer needs, which is achieved by creating products that solve problems and improve the lives of customers.

By focusing on customer needs, businesses can develop products that are relevant and valuable to their target audience. This requires a deep understanding of the customer, including their pain points, challenges, and desires. By listening to customer feedback and conducting market research, businesses can identify customer needs and create products that address those needs in innovative ways.

Building a product that solves customer problems can result in several benefits. First, it can increase customer satisfaction and loyalty, as customers are more likely to return to a company that has provided them with a solution to their problem. This can lead to increased revenue, as satisfied customers are more likely to become repeat customers and recommend the product to others.

Additionally, focusing on customer needs can result in increased innovation and differentiation. By understanding customer needs and pain points, businesses can create unique products that stand out from competitors and provide a competitive advantage. This can lead to increased market share and growth opportunities for the business.

Furthermore, meeting customer needs can help businesses build trust and credibility with their customers. When a business delivers a high-quality product that solves a customer's problem, it demonstrates a commitment to customer satisfaction and quality, which can enhance the brand reputation and lead to increased customer loyalty.

In conclusion, meeting customer needs, or solving problems, is a critical core value for building a strong and quality product. By creating products that solve customer problems, businesses can increase customer satisfaction, drive innovation and differentiation, build trust and credibility, and ultimately achieve long-term success.

Stands Out In The Market (Visibility, Outstanding)

Standing out in the market can be a core value for building a strong and quality product because it differentiates a company's offering from its competitors and creates a unique selling proposition. When a product stands out in the market, it attracts attention and generates interest from potential customers, leading to increased sales and revenue.

To stand out in the market, a company must focus on creating a product that not only meets but exceeds customer expectations. This requires a commitment to quality and a willingness to invest in research and development to innovate and improve the product. By doing so, a company can create a unique product that offers superior value to customers and distinguishes itself from competitors.

Additionally, standing out in the market can also lead to increased brand recognition and awareness, which are essential for building a strong and successful business. When a product is unique and memorable, it can generate positive word-of-mouth advertising and customer loyalty, leading to repeat business and long-term success.

Furthermore, standing out in the market can also enable a company to charge a premium price for its product, as customers are willing to pay more for products that they perceive as high-quality and unique. This can increase profit margins and provide resources to invest in further research and development to maintain the product's competitive edge.

In summary, standing out in the market is a core value for building a strong and quality product as it differentiates a company's offering from its competitors, generates customer interest and loyalty, increases brand recognition and awareness enables premium pricing and provides resources for further innovation and growth.

Provides Value to The Business (Revenue)

To genuinely generate revenue for any business is a core value for building a strong and quality product because revenue is the lifeblood of any business. A product that genuinely generates revenue is one that meets the needs of its target market, delivers value, and creates a positive customer experience.

When a business focuses on building a strong and quality product that genuinely generates revenue, it prioritizes meeting customer needs and wants. This, in turn, leads to increased customer satisfaction, repeat business, and positive word-of-mouth advertising. Customers are more likely to purchase products that solve a problem, meet a need, or fulfill a desire, and a quality product can do just that.

Moreover, a product that genuinely generates revenue can provide a sustainable source of income for a business. It can create a stable foundation for growth and expansion, allowing the business to invest in research and development, marketing, and other essential activities. This can enable the business to remain relevant in the market, compete with other businesses, and ultimately achieve long-term success.

In contrast, a product that does not genuinely generate revenue can be a drain on resources and hinder business growth. Poor quality products, products that do not meet customer needs, or products that fail to create a positive customer experience can lead to decreased sales, negative customer reviews, and harm the brand's reputation. This can result in lost revenue, decreased market share, and ultimately lead to business failure.

In conclusion, building a strong and quality product that genuinely generates revenue is a core value for any business. It prioritizes meeting customer needs and wants, leads to increased customer satisfaction, and creates a sustainable source of income. By focusing on revenue generation as a core value, a business can lay the foundation for long-term success, growth, and profitability.

CHAPTER 2

BUILDING FOR THE FUTURE

In all your buildings, if they do not strategically suggest sustainable growth into the future, you have failed before starting. We cannot overemphasize that building for the future requires a focus on innovation, adaptability, and very importantly, continuous improvement to ensure that a business can meet the changing demands of the marketplace and remain competitive in the long run. By investing in the right resources, talent, and infrastructure, companies can build a solid foundation for future success and create lasting value for stakeholders.

From the foregoing, it is not out of place to say that building for the future refers to the act of making long-term investments and strategic decisions for sustainable and resilient systems, structures, and processes that can withstand the challenges and uncertainties of the future. This approach requires a forward-thinking mind-set that considers the potential impacts of future trends, technologies, and events, as well as the social, economic, and environmental factors that could affect the longevity and success of a given project or initiative.

Building for the future is not only essential for ensuring the long-term viability and success of individual projects or organizations, but also for creating a more equitable, just, and sustainable world for future generations. So it is clear and evident that whatsoever path an entrepreneur takes, it has direct and indirect consequences not only on him/her but the general public. Hence, the need to be proactively involved in the future as much as the present. By adopting a proactive, holistic, and inclusive approach to planning and decision-making, we can build stronger, more resilient, and more adaptive systems that can withstand the challenges and opportunities of a rapidly changing market and world.

CHAPTER 3

QUALITY PRODUCTS NATURALLY ATTRACT INVESTMENTS

In a recent conversation with a young entrepreneur seeking my advice on how to secure funding for their start-up, I offered a simple suggestion: "focus on developing a quality product that is credible, solid, and sellable." I explained that investors are naturally attracted to products that have the potential to succeed in the marketplace and that the viability of a product is what really matters when it comes to securing investment. When you have a product, you do not panic about capitals

Quality products have the ability to generate excitement and interest among investors because they offer a clear value proposition and a strong competitive advantage. When a product is credible, solid, and sellable, it demonstrates to investors that the business is well-positioned for success and has a clear understanding of the needs of the market and the people.

Investors want to see for themselves that your business has a solid plan for success and that the product being offered is a key component of that plan. A quality product helps to build trust and confidence with investors, who are more likely to provide funding when they believe in the potential of the product and the team behind it.

Ultimately, the key to attracting investments is to focus on developing a quality, solid, credible, and viable product that meets the needs of the market and offers a clear value proposition. By doing so, entrepreneurs can generate interest and excitement among investors, and position themselves for success in the long term.

CHAPTER 4

AVOIDING COMMON PITFALLS

Building a quality product that can stand the test of time is key to the success of any business. However, there are common pitfalls that can undermine the quality of a product, and ultimately lead to failure. Here are some tips for avoiding these pitfalls and building a quality product that can stand the test of time:

Understand The Needs of The Market

Before developing a product, it is important to conduct market research to understand the needs and preferences of potential customers. This will help to ensure that the product meets a real need in the marketplace, and has the potential to succeed.

Focus on Usability and User Experience

A product that is difficult to use or offers a poor user experience is unlikely to be successful. Therefore, it is important to focus on usability and user experience throughout the development process and to incorporate feedback from users to improve the product over time.

Invest In Quality Materials/Resources And Components

A quality product is only as good as its materials and components. Therefore, it is important to invest in high-quality materials and components that can withstand wear and tear, and that will not compromise the safety or reliability of the product.

Test, Test, Test

Testing is an essential part of the product development process and should be conducted at every stage to ensure that the product is functioning as intended and that it meets the needs of users. This includes everything from user testing to stress testing and should be done rigorously to identify any potential issues before the product goes to market.

Focus on Continuous Improvement

Building a quality product is an ongoing process, and requires a commitment to continuous improvement. This includes incorporating feedback from users, monitoring performance metrics, and making adjustments as needed to ensure that the product continues to meet the needs of the market.

CHAPTER 5

LESSONS FROM SUCCESSFUL ENTREPRENEURS

We have lots of valuable insights and lessons from successful entrepreneurs globally and locally that can help inspire and guide aspiring business leaders/owners today. For the purpose of this write-up, let us consider some of the lessons;

Pursue Your Passion

Successful entrepreneurs are often driven by a deep passion for what they do. By pursuing a passion and building a business around it, entrepreneurs can find fulfillment and purpose in their work. For example, Sara Blakely, the founder of Spanx, has said that her passion for creating comfortable and flattering undergarments inspired her to start her business.

Embrace Failure

Failure is a natural part of the entrepreneurial journey, it is not a bad thing, and successful entrepreneurs understand that it is often necessary to fail in order to learn and grow. Rather than being discouraged by failure, entrepreneurs should embrace it as an opportunity to learn, pivot, and improve. The likes of Elon Musk, founder of SpaceX, has said that failure is an essential part of the process of innovation and that it is important to take risks and learn from mistakes.

Build A Strong Team

No entrepreneur can succeed alone, and building a strong team is critical to the success of any business. Successful entrepreneurs focus on hiring talented, motivated individuals who share their vision and are committed to helping the business grow. Jeff Bezos, the founder of Amazon, has emphasized the importance of hiring people who are smarter than you, and who can bring new perspectives and ideas to the table.

Focus on Customer Experience

Tony Hsieh, the former CEO of Zappos, built his business around the principle of delivering exceptional customer service/experience, and this focus on the customer helped to differentiate Zappos from its competitors. Indeed, the most successful businesses prioritize the customer experience above all else, because as the saying goes, *the customer is king.* By understanding the needs and preferences of customers, and providing them with a seamless, enjoyable experience, entrepreneurs can build a loyal customer base that will help to sustain the business over the long term.

Persistency

Building a successful business takes time, effort, and perseverance, and successful entrepreneurs are often characterized by their persistence and resilience in the face of challenges and setbacks. Oprah Winfrey, media mogul and founder of OWN, consistently spoke about the importance of persistence and determination in achieving success.

Transparency

Transparency is another important lesson that can be learned from successful entrepreneurs. Being transparent with customers and stakeholders can help to build trust, establish credibility, and demonstrate a commitment to quality and integrity. By being transparent about their business practices, entrepreneurs can differentiate themselves from competitors and build a loyal customer base that values transparency and honesty.

Entrepreneurial Ecosystems

Successful Nigerian entrepreneurs, in the likes of Tony Elumelu, founder of the *Tony Elumelu Foundation*, Mitchell Elegbe, the founder and CEO of Interswitch, a leading African payments and technology company, Iyinoluwa Aboyeji, a Nigerian entrepreneur and investor who co-founded Andela, a company that trains and deploys software developers across Africa; also the founder of Future Africa, an investment platform that supports African start-ups and a host of others have all emphasized the importance of building strong entrepreneurial ecosystems, including mentorship, funding, and supportive policies. The mentioned names have written their names indelibly in the history book for advocating and building entrepreneurship in Africa, providing mentorship and funding to thousands of African entrepreneurs.

Resilience

Entrepreneurs in Nigeria often face significant challenges, including a difficult business environment and lack of infrastructure, unforeseen government regulations, and policies. Successful entrepreneurs are often characterized by their resilience in the face of these challenges, finding ways to overcome obstacles and succeed. Aliko Dangote, the founder of the Dangote Group, for instance, built a multi-billion dollar conglomerate in Nigeria, despite the cacophonous challenges in the country's business environment.

Above all, successful entrepreneurs have a range of qualities and traits that contribute to their success, including passion, resilience, innovation, and a focus on the customer. By embodying these principles and learning from the examples of successful entrepreneurs, aspiring business leaders can position themselves for success in their own ventures.

Forbes refers to Tony Elumelu as *power builder*, and Dangote the *richest man in Africa*

CHAPTER 6

LESSONS FOR YOUNG ENTREPRENEURS

Apparently, we cannot end this piece without recommending some lessons that young entrepreneurs can learn to help them become more prepared to build enduring products for high performance. Here are a few key points:

Be Resilient

Starting a business is a challenging endeavour and it is important to be prepared for setbacks and obstacles. Successful entrepreneurs often emphasize the importance of resilience in the face of challenges.

Focus on Solving a Problem

Many successful businesses are built around solving a specific problem or meeting a specific need. As a young entrepreneur, it is important to identify a problem or need that you're passionate about and develop a solution that meets that need.

Build A Strong Team

No entrepreneur can succeed on their own. Building a strong team is essential for success. This includes finding partners, employees, and advisors who can help support and guide you on your entrepreneurial journey.

Embrace Failure

Failure is a natural part of the entrepreneurial journey. Successful entrepreneurs often embrace failure as a learning opportunity and use it to iterate and improve their business.

Seek Mentorship and Guidance

Learning from others who have gone before you is a valuable way to gain insights and avoid common pitfalls. Seek mentors and advisors who can provide guidance and support.

Be Adaptable

The business landscape is constantly evolving and it is important to be adaptable and flexible in response to changing circumstances. Successful entrepreneurs are often able to pivot and adjust their business model as needed to stay competitive.

Overall, these are just a few of the many lessons that young entrepreneurs can learn from successful entrepreneurs. By embracing these lessons and learning from the experiences of others, young entrepreneurs can increase their chances of success in the world of business.

CHAPTER 7

QUALITY PRODUCT AND BRAND REPUTATION

Quality plays a vital role in shaping a brand's reputation and overall success. A company's product or service is a direct reflection of its brand and has the potential to influence customer loyalty, perception, and sales. In today's highly competitive market, businesses must prioritize quality to remain relevant and competitive.

The relationship between quality and brand reputation is symbiotic. High-quality products and services contribute to a positive brand reputation, while a strong brand reputation can drive sales and boost customer loyalty. Companies that prioritize quality in their products and services are more likely to build trust with their customers, leading to increased sales and repeat business.

A solid product is essential for business growth as it can differentiate a brand from its competitors. A company that consistently delivers quality products or services can create a competitive advantage and increase customer satisfaction, leading to increased market share and revenue growth. Additionally, a reputation for quality can attract new customers and improve brand awareness, allowing businesses to expand their customer base and reach new markets.

On the other hand, poor-quality products or services can damage a brand's reputation and have significant financial consequences. Negative customer reviews recalls, and lawsuits can lead to decreased sales, increased costs, and harm a brand's reputation. A negative reputation can also impact a company's ability to attract new customers and retain existing ones.

Summarily, a solid product is quintessential for business growth in the following way;

Builds Trust and Loyalty: Quality products can help build trust and loyalty with customers, leading to repeat business and positive word-of-mouth advertising.

Differentiates from Competitors: A company that consistently delivers high-quality products can differentiate itself from competitors and create a competitive advantage in the market.

Increases Sales: Customers are willing to pay more for products that they perceive as high-quality, which can lead to increased sales and revenue growth.

Enhances Brand Reputation: A reputation for quality can attract new customers and improve brand awareness, leading to increased market share and business growth.

Reduces Costs: Investing in quality products can reduce costs associated with returns, repairs, and customer complaints, ultimately improving the bottom line.

Enables Innovation: High-quality products can enable a company to innovate and develop new products, leading to continued growth and success in the market.

From the foregoing, it is clear that a solid product is essential for business growth as it can help build trust and loyalty with customers, differentiate a company from its competitors, increase sales and revenue, enhance brand reputation, reduce costs, and enable innovation.

In conclusion, quality is a critical component of a brand's reputation and business growth. Companies must prioritize quality in their products and services to build trust, increase customer loyalty, and differentiate themselves from competitors. A commitment to quality can result in increased sales, market share, and long-term success for businesses.

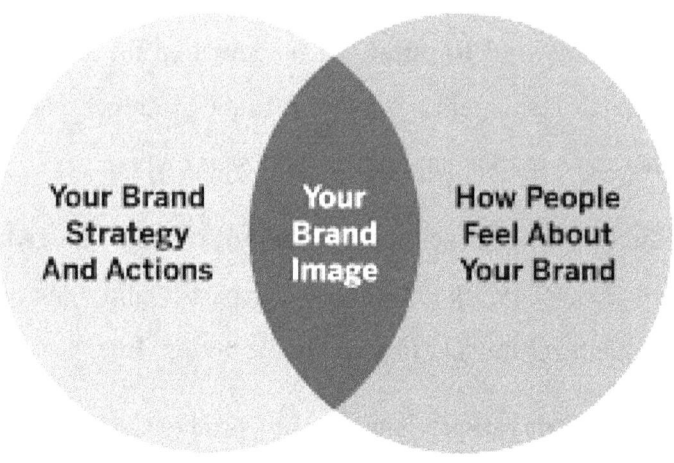

ABOUT THE AUTHOR

Phelyx David is a multifaceted author with a diverse academic background. With bachelor's degrees in Philosophy and Theology from the University of Ibadan and the Pontifical Urban University, Rome, respectively, Phelyx's areas of expertise span from logical reasoning and psychology to scriptural interpretation and moral theology.

In addition to his academic credentials, Phelyx is a senior manager and accomplished leader in the FinTech corporate space. He uses his wealth of knowledge and experience to write thought-provoking pieces on existential realities, advocacy for human psychological well-being, spirituality, and business. His publications offer a unique perspective, blending philosophical and theological insights with practical applications in the corporate world.

www.ingramcontent.com/pod-product-compliance
Lightning Source LLC
Chambersburg PA
CBHW071146220526
45467CB00015B/2026